# Honesty Box

## Poetry & Prose

Written by

Carlos Harleaux

HONESTY BOX
Copyright ©2014 by Carlos Harleaux

Published by 7th Sign Publishing
(www.PeauxeticExpressions.com)

All rights reserved. No part of this book may be reproduced or transmitted in any form or by any means without written permission from the author.

ISBN 978-0-9890767-0-8

Book Cover Design and Illustrations by Desmond Blair (www.blairmediadigital.com)

Photography by Terri Butcher (W Photography)

## Thanks and Dedication

I'm extremely blessed to have my third book completed in three years! But there is no way I could have done any of this on my own. First and foremost, I have to thank God for gifting me with the ability to express myself through poetry. He has allowed me to channel a lot of energy that could have been negative into something positive.

I also want to give thanks to my parents, Debra and Ronnie Swisher and Carl Harleaux. Your endless love and support over the years has truly kept and continues to keep me moving. I'm so honored to have great parents like you.

To my beautiful wife, Alex. Your love, patience and encouragement are immeasurable. Thank you for being my love and my help.

Thanks to John Adams for being a great brother, creative force, and being the first author to believe in 7th Sign Publishing. You took a chance that most people would not have and I'm very grateful for it. Shirley Thomas, thank you for believing in 7th Sign as well, with the release of your debut book. I'm elated that you chose me to help turn your dreams into reality.

Desmond Blair, thanks for creating this awesome cover. Your gift is amazing and I'm proud to call you my brother.

To all of my family and friends who are too numerous to specifically name here, I love you all and thank you more than words could ever say.

Last, but definitely not least….thank YOU, the reader! I could not continue to release books without your support, feedback, comments, and inspiration to write another line, thought or stanza.

I dedicate *Honesty Box* to the memory of my maternal grandmother, Jean "Granny" Kyle. Your love and tight hugs will always be with me and your witty, comical kind of honesty still brings a smile to my face. I love you.

Now, let's take a look and see what's inside the box…..

## Thanks and Dedication

I'm extremely blessed to have my third book completed in three years! But there is no way I could have done any of this on my own. First and foremost, I have to thank God for gifting me with the ability to express myself through poetry. He has allowed me to channel a lot of energy that could have been negative into something positive.

I also want to give thanks to my parents, Debra and Ronnie Swisher and Carl Harleaux. Your endless love and support over the years has truly kept and continues to keep me moving. I'm so honored to have great parents like you.

To my beautiful wife, Alex. Your love, patience and encouragement are immeasurable. Thank you for being my love and my help.

Thanks to John Adams for being a great brother, creative force, and being the first author to believe in 7th Sign Publishing. You took a chance that most people would not have and I'm very grateful for it. Shirley Thomas, thank you for believing in 7th Sign as well, with the release of your debut book. I'm elated that you chose me to help turn your dreams into reality.

Desmond Blair, thanks for creating this awesome cover. Your gift is amazing and I'm proud to call you my brother.

To all of my family and friends who are too numerous to specifically name here, I love you all and thank you more than words could ever say.

Last, but definitely not least….thank YOU, the reader! I could not continue to release books without your support, feedback, comments, and inspiration to write another line, thought or stanza.

I dedicate *Honesty Box* to the memory of my maternal grandmother, Jean "Granny" Kyle. Your love and tight hugs will always be with me and your witty, comical kind of honesty still brings a smile to my face. I love you.

Now, let's take a look and see what's inside the box…..

## Introduction

I've had the name of this book (as well as my first two books, *Blurred Vision* and *Hindsight 20/20*) in my head for several years now. It's funny how the most uncomfortable, shocking and unexpected moments in our lives lay the foundation for our greatest inspiration. True to form, an incident happened a few years ago that gave me the title and concept behind this very book you have in front of you. Many of you may remember a once popular Facebook application called 'Honesty Box'. Honesty Box was a way to anonymously tell people what you really thought about them (be it good or bad). A blue message meant it was from a guy and a pink message meant it was from a woman. One particular "blue" message I received definitely threw me for a loop.

I can't remember the message verbatim. I should have saved it and put it in here, but I digress. The message was from someone who supposedly was a close friend of mine. Their comment basically stated that I had changed (and not for the good) and a list of other things that they felt made me less of a person. At first, I was pissed. Then I got over it and it actually became funny to me. I never found out who the person was that sent me the message, and after a while I stopped caring about it. But I have to thank them because they helped give me a creative spark that has exploded....years later.

Social media outlets have in a sense made us cowards. We say what we feel, but behind the comfort of screens of cell phones and computers. Don't get me wrong, there's nothing wrong with expressing your feelings and if you have to resort to anonymous outlets, at least doing it in private is the way to go. But whatever happened to old fashioned arguments? You know, giving people a piece of your mind face to face. I guess that's outdated now. Nevertheless, the collection of poems and essays you are about to read are my take on the 'Honesty Box'. It's my truth, from my perspective, and I'm sticking to it. I hope it inspires you to unlock your own honesty box, or help someone else unlock theirs.

# Table of Contents

Introduction

Anonymous
Cover Girl
Inside Out
Turn Me Inside Out*
Lasso
Entangled
Forever
Crumbs
One Hand In My Pocket

They'll Watch Us Glow*
Glow
Pretty Pedestal
Stained
Apprehension
Free Smells (Don't Need Em)*
Crash The Waves
I'll Toast To That
Running Marathons
Going Home*
Walking on the Clouds

Hands Up
Did I Do That?
The One That Got Away*
Blow Out The Candles
Am I The Only One?
Remove Your Cool*
Decisions
I Love You Only…
Heart Surgeon

Not Oblivious

A Woman Named Joy*
Jealous Guys
Principality
Doormat
Open Secrets
Let's Play 'I Never'*
Giving You The Finger *
Tastes Like
Believer
We Will Laugh
Let My Shadow Be Enough
Up The Latter
Swerving In My Lane*
When The Screaming Stops
The Things We Never Said
Slick Intuition

No M.A.M.*
Phantom On the Run Neglecting (PORN)
Snap Your Fingers
Pull These Strings
Wonder Years
Your Hood Won't Save You
Just Between Me And You *
Honesty Box
Not Amused
Dead End Street
That Self $!^t

I Might Be
Good Thing I Don't….
By Invitation Only*
Drip Drop Floods*
Forever Ain't Far
N2MeUC
One Up*
Insomniac

Wipped
Better You Than Me*
Beautiful Trouble
Pillow Talk
Check Your DM (Direct Message)
Smooth Skin
Quicksand
Why We Lie
Keep Your Fame

*Denotes original essays

# Honesty Bit #1

Most people will not tell you what they really think about you to your face. If you ever get the privilege of receiving such information from an individual, respect it (be it positive or negative) whether you like it or not.

## Anonymous

So you've finally got balls
What took you so long?
Stepping out of your deceptive shadows
With your shameful cloak in tow
Sweeping the floor
I should applaud you for being so brave
But I won't
My hands wouldn't dare
Kill the beautiful space
Betwixt them…on….you
As a matter of fact
I'll scrap the last few lines
That began to trickle down
From thought to pen
To fingers to paper
All in the name of
An anonymous hater

## Cover Girl

She's flawlessly magnificent
And telling all these bitches to bow down
Airbrushed for delectable obsession
Tweaked, twerked, flipped, cut, nipped, tucked
To perfection
Never seen an ass like that
That's because there isn't really an ass like that
Or hips or breasts and thighs
Or lips or legs or eyes, oh my
Cowardly robots programmed
To cease the search for their hearts
And pick up the torch to lead them
Down the road just to play a part
That eventually fades into materialistic abyss
Oh yes, those breasts will droop
That ass will sag
That smile will drag into a frown….eventually
When you realize you've dropped your crown
And then have the nerve to
Want him to treat you like royalty
He won't….
You're parallel to the ground
And have lost your shine
For what? I hope it was worth it
At least you were a cover girl
They can't take that away from you….

## Inside Out

To the naked eye it seems
Like it would be easy to be
Tied up in these shoes
But if you take a closer look
You would see these damn unpretty
Crooked smiles painted picture perfectly
And ever so stiffly across my face
Plastered over disasters
No one seems to notice
Perhaps it's because they are
Unrecognizable even to me
Or maybe they simply don't care
Honestly, if you flipped me inside out
Turned me upside down
Until the change and everything
Came falling from my pockets
Would you still love me?
Would you still think I'm cool?
Would I still be worthy of your high praise?
That never should have been given to me
In the first place
If they flipped us all inside out
What would they see?
Would it be the ugliness in our beauty or
The beauty in what we think is ugly?

## Turn Me Inside Out

You think you know, but you have no idea. That person you see at the gym that is the epitome of how you want to look. Ah....but there's one small thing you can't see to factor in. They go home at night and throw up everything they've eaten that day. That couple that you see that seems so perfect. That's just it. Things aren't always as they seem. She is a victim of domestic abuse, but lucky for her there's make up for that. That exec's position that you so desire to have one day. Their title gleams brighter than the sun. But you're so blinded by their status that you don't notice the 4 bottles of prescription pills they have in their desk drawer to cope with the stress. There's one thing all of these people have in common. Even we can find similarities with them. We look good on the outside, but do our insides always match what the mirror shows? Sometimes we have to look a little deeper for the real truth.

Often times we look at people and our vision is blurred by those things that appeal to the flesh. We see the pretty face, suit and tie, luxury car, beautiful home, and money in the bank. Is there anything wrong that? No! We should look our best and go after what we desire. But what happens after you gain everything tangible that you've ever wanted? Is it actually worth it when we get it? Do we judge others based on their outer appearance with no clue as to what's really going on behind closed doors? Are we envious of others because of what they have, not realizing the hell they go through to get it and keep it? What would we see if we were flipped inside out? Would the reflection of our inner being be unrecognizable even to us?

Remember when you were a kid and you used to flip your eyelids to scare people? Ok, so maybe it was just me that did that. As adults, we learn that it's not "cool" to let people see those things that we perceive to be ugly. We think it devalues us as a person or makes us less than somebody else. In reality, we all have something that's ugly on the inside that we may not be so proud of. Or maybe even something on the outside that we don't like. But that doesn't have to mean it's the end of the world. The things we ignore will never be corrected.

So go ahead, flip yourself inside out. You just may be surprised at what you see.

## Lasso

Whip it really fast and
Raise it high above my head
Contemplating carefully
Just where I'll let it land
I can hear the rope cutting
Through the silent screams
Of the mess I've made
That's so transparent to me
Yet invisible to others
And that's just it
If I could lasso
Your heartache and capture it
Forevermore
I would
If I could reign in that
Raging bull and calm it
Like a sleepy baby
You know I would
If I could tuck away
All the hurtful words
I didn't mean to say
Inside the brim of my hat
Or slash them on the
Spurs of my heel, I would
Bury it all in the hay stack
Smaller than a grain of sand
If I could I'd capture it
And use this lasso to
Pull it all back

# Entangled

I am caught and suspended in mid air
It's magical, elastic
How our love only grows stronger
Over and under any obstacles
And through and to a higher level
And I thank you
For coming with me
Even when it may be difficult
Even when the rain has come
You are the sunshine
I feel I am entitled to
A love like this
I never knew
Beautifully stunning
Amazingly breathtaking
The way I feel
When I look at you
I am entangled, elated
And don't want to break free
Thank you for giving
Your very best to me

## Forever

Forever…I love you
Though I've never seen your face
I love your mystery
Such a distant entity
Though I can reach out
And just barely touch your skin
Forever…you are stubborn
And march to the beat of your own drum
Keeping time with your own metronome
That often feels out of sync from ours
Forever…I ask you boldly
For what only you can see
And you just respond with whispers
Ever so softly
Forever…I hate the way you lie
You promise and then you break it
We value you and say that
We cherish you, but live so recklessly
Taking for granted that you will
Safely cradle our existence in your arms
For infinite years to come
Oh forever….I love you
But why are you so complicated?

# Crumbs

I've been surviving on these crumbs
For quite a while now
But now I'm starting to get hunger pains
And I'm about to show my fangs
The sun is slowly setting
Blending orange and purple hues
Bon appetite
Was it ever my game to lose?
Salivating over sweet aromas
That I have yet to fully taste
Tired of catching the left overs
Falling from your plate
My energy is waning
The lack of sustenance is draining
My vitals are being swallowed in the shadows
That is until you feel
It's time to resuscitate me
But this time I'm wiping the last crumb
From the corner of my lips
This table is turning…literally
Now you will eat from the floor
Now you will struggle and beg
For what you should have given me….freely
Without coercion
Maybe someone else will come along
And help sweep you up with all the crumbs

## One Hand In My Pocket

My knees buckle as
I make my way to stand
Decisions, decisions
This envelope is sealed, but it's not too late
For me to rip it open and slickly slide
This forty five right back in my pocket
Yeah that's what I'll do
Cause I have too many bills
Too many needs
Not enough time in between these checks
That I have to put up with too much ish…
(oops) Forgot where I was for a second
To only get 90%
I have too many wants unfulfilled
Truth be told
This is the real reason
Why I tip toe outside when it's time to give
Shhhh….we'll keep this as our secret
Spank each other's hands and say
That's not the way to live
So I give from my net, since
That's all I get to see
Gross negligence
From what He could have
Easily taken away from me
And I thank Him
That's why I've got one hand in the air
Waving a humbling thanks
And the other is in my pocket
And that's where it shall stay
Y'all pray for me…with both hands please

## Honesty Bit #2

Never walk into a room (or into adversity) with your head down. It implies that you're already defeated.

## They'll Watch Us Glow

Imagine walking down a dark dirt road that's full of potholes. You miss a couple, stumble over a few and then....BOOM! There's no way you could have dodged this one. You fall so hard that you must have broken your leg or at least severely twisted your ankle. How will you ever get out of this mess? Just when you think there is no other option but to give up, you notice someone running on the side of the road in the distance. There's something shining in their hand. A closer look shows that it's a glow stick. Finally....a sign of relief as you call out for help! We all are representatives of the glow stick. Many of us are in a season of trouble, leaving one or about to enter one. Don't think so? Keep waking up....it's on the way. But don't pull out your pessimistic "Woe is me" T-Shirt just yet. There's something magical about being broken.

If you've ever seen an unused glow stick, then you know it has to be broken before it lights up. And not just a little break. The break usually has to be applied with some elbow grease in order for the fluid inside to illuminate. The stronger the blow, the brighter the glow. Isn't that crazy? Something that was once considered whole is being brought down to size and crushed to literally light up the sky. Perhaps, we could learn a lot more from the glow stick than just using it outdoors at night, for a party or for a concert. For starters, even though the glow stick has to be broken to work properly, it can be returned to an upright position (thank goodness). When we're going through our struggles it's easy to think that we'll never be what we used to be. But in order to get to the light, we have to get through the brokenness.

Has it ever crossed our minds that maybe our brokenness was not even meant for us? Maybe we had to be broken so that others could see us glow and avoid the same mistakes that we made. Plus, if we weren't around during the breaking process, we just know that it happened and now there is light. Everyone doesn't have to know the gritty details of your story to appreciate your glow.  Just knowing there is a story is enough.  Does this mean that we should all run out and find ways to be broken to shine from within???  Of course not.  Brokenness will come on its own without any prompting.  But it does mean that the darkest hour is only 60 minutes and there's a florescent light waiting to be revealed……literally just around the bend.

## Watch Us Glow

Right now they see our dimly lit light
Holding their applause for gossip and lies
And holding their breaths
Waiting for the great fall
Then pick us up but only
After they watch us crawl
They see right through our smiles
Or so they think
And diagnose the pain
In denial of their own hurt
Ha ha and yet they think they've gained
They see us coming from afar
At a non-threatening distance
Too far to leave a scar
But get too close and see our stars
Shine so brightly that their eyes squint
And burn in disbelief
Illuminating all of the deep, dark
Ignorance in your soul
Didn't want to respect our light before?
Now you'll be forced to watch us glow
Turn on the lights
And don't reach for your shades
It's blinding, we know
And there's nowhere for you to go
Sit back and revel in the glow

## Pretty Pedestal

I wish that you would
Get me down from here
These heights are making me nauseous
And there's nowhere to go
Above or beneath here
I make you smile today
Because I embody the elevated dream
You have contrived in your mind
But when I make you cry tomorrow
I lose my equilibrium
Because I'm not what you imagined
So go ahead
Get it over with
Kick this stand from under me
Because I can't bear to live
Another day on your pretty pedestal
So kick it down now
Don't worry about the fall
Bring me back to Earth
Where I belong
Pedestals never last
No matter how beautiful we make them
So please kick me down
And watch me fall……to you

## Stained

You think you're so pristine
And cleaner than most
Without a spectacle of dirt
Don't overestimate your worth
Because if I pull this black light
Out my back pocket
We'll see all your flaws
And stains and sins
That you think we can't see
Yet you blame it on me
Manipulation and deceit
We were bought with a price
So show me your receipt
That's what I thought
These crickets are chirping
Can you hear them?
Shhhh...the silence
Removing the masks from the thieves
Taking the sheets off the fornicators
Yet you're a perpetrator
Pretending to be something you're clearly not
Ooh there's a grey dot and a red spot
And a blue hue on your white suit
Do you really want me to
Reveal the truth
And pull this black light out my pocket?
Stand in line and fall in form
We're all stained to imperfection
And contrary to your warped beliefs
You are no exception

## Apprehension

I try my best to believe you and
Rest assured that this time will be different
Paranoia nagging at my neck
Skepticism scratching at my heels
So forgive me if what you say
Goes in one ear and out of the other
Don't mind me if I wait for your actions instead
Only there is where I'll receive confirmation
Forgive me for being apprehensive
But you've never given me a reason to
Dive into your truth
Oh wait there was that one time
But I'll just wade over here
In waters I can see
You won't trick me this time
By bringing me out to the deep end
Only leaving me to find my own way home
I want to believe you, really I do
But this little pebble in my shoe called
Apprehension
Won't let me walk that road with you

## Free Smells (Don't Need Em)

It's amazing how much social media has grown since the introduction of "The Honesty Box" on Facebook. Back then, the site was still trying to find its niche, MySpace was starting to fizzle out and Twitter had not become the major force it is today. We can forget about Instagram. We had no idea what that was back then either. Somewhere along the way with all of the modern technological advances, selfies, instant uploads and frequent status updates; we became increasingly transparent as well. Think about it. How many times have you seen someone tag themselves at the gym and update everyone on their friends list of how much they're "killing it" in their workout? Smart….now everyone knows your routine and when they can come by and break in your house since you're at the gym every night at 7:00 pm. But I digress…

Not only do we sometimes post frivolous messages (everything short of –and at times including- "I'm on the toilet now"), but we also air out all of our dirty laundry. There must be some secret code out there that says the more drama, profanity and sexual references your page has, it will garner more attention. Well….sadly to say in this day and age, that's not far from the truth. The more risqué, shocking and explicit, the better. Have we ever stopped to think that some things we really shouldn't see (or care to see for that matter)?

There's something to be said for a certain level of privacy and dignity. We honestly have lost a lot of that in the mix of the social media whirlwind. I enjoy getting on Facebook, Twitter, Instagram and any other social media site just like the next person, but there are some aspects of my life I wouldn't ever feel comfortable posting for the whole world to see. For those that are comfortable with it, that's ok if it works for them. We should all just make sure we're being led by our own values and beliefs, not what the masses of the social media stratosphere are doing.

## Crash The Waves

This water keeps rising
Past my shoulders and to my ears
My eyes are just above the current
Feeling weighted down with doubt and fear
I kick and push and rise and stroke
To stay above water
And get back to the shore
Drifting further to the depths of the sea
But the sun is still shining
So I've got that on my side
And I'll just use the tide to carry me
Position my being to conquer the next storm
I'll stand tall
You'll see me just beneath the sky
Crashing the waves
And riding safely in to solid ground

## I'll Toast To That

If I'm causing you so much pain
Then it's insanity for you to stay
We wouldn't want that now, would we?
We've been down that road time and time again
So if it brings a smile to your face
A pep in your step
A jolt in your spine to stand up tall
A lift from gravity to cushion your fall
A life jacket to help you stay afloat
An extra oar to paddle your boat
A round of applause for validation
A catalyst to spark the you you never were
A jump start sprint to the rest of your life
A roller coaster thrill
As you ascend before the drop
A revelation of the last days
That see you on your own
Then who am I to interfere?
Let's just chalk it up to life
And toast to your freedom

# Running Marathons

With you pushing me
Somehow I can take one more step
Embrace the pavement
And believe I can take it one more day
Because you've been there
To quench my most thirsty moments
Of extreme dehydration
The wings to help me fly to
Euphoric levitation
I can run on a little longer
I can go a little further
Just your smile makes me stronger
Like I could run marathons
Forever and ever
I could run marathons
And leave my fears in the distant dust
I could run marathons
Without a single gasp for air
I can see the finish line
With you, I feel like I'm already there

# Going Home

Tuesday, February 25, 2014. The time had to have been around 6:45 pm. I decided to call my grandmother because I hadn't talked to her in a little while. The last time I physically saw her was exactly two months before then, on Christmas day. She had gotten very ill right before my birthday. But when she answered the phone, I had high hopes that her health would make a 360 degree turn. We only talked for a few minutes, but sometimes I wish I could press rewind to have that time back again. She was laughing and sounded upbeat, although I could tell she was still battling some physical pain. I asked her how she was feeling and she said, "Better today than the last couple of days". I proceeded to ask her more questions because I was concerned for her health. She stopped me before I could continue and asked, "Well baby how are you? How's my girl (my wife)?"

I told her that I was doing well and was just at school a little early before my night class. She responded and said, "Oh that's good then. Just remember to slow down sometimes." I tried to swing the conversation back to her, but she wouldn't allow it. I didn't understand how she could be in that much pain and so concerned about how I was doing. We exchanged "I love you's" and that was the last time I spoke with her. I was planning on going to visit her that same weekend….but never got the chance. On Thursday, February 27, 2014, I got the call from my mother that she had passed. I was angered and saddened when I initially heard the news. I selfishly thought, "God, why couldn't she have just held on until I got to see her!?" That reason I don't know, but I had to realize that she was no longer in pain or suffering. She was free. Out of our entire conversation, 2 words stood out the most to me: "Slow down".

So what's the purpose of me sharing this with you? We live in such a fast paced world that it's so easy to get carried away with to do lists, personal hobbies and paying bills. But if we don't remember to slow down to take it all in, we'll never enjoy life. I truly thank my grandmother for the reminder. I wonder if she even knew how much that short conversation would even impact me. I miss her and still have my moments of sadness, but in slowing down I realized a divine sign became visible for me. I don't believe in luck or even numerology to its full extent. But I do believe that numbers hold a certain power.

There are two numbers that have been very significant in my life, especially in the last ten years or so: 7 and 9. 7 represents completion and perfection. This is part of the reason I decided to name my publishing company $7^{th}$ Sign Publishing. It also stemmed from my line's name, The $7^{th}$ Sign of Completion, when I was initiated into Alpha Phi Alpha Fraternity, Inc. The last time I talked my grandmother was on the $25^{th}$ day of the month. 2 + 5 = 7. Her life was nearing completion then. My parents' address, my grandparents' address and every residence I've lived at on my own in Dallas all equal 9. 9 has come to mean a feeling of comfort for me; something that feels natural and right at home. My grandmother passed on the $27^{th}$ day of the month. 2 + 7 = 9. She's home….resting now. I thank her for reminding me to slow down and pay attention to the things in life that really matter.

## Walking on the Clouds

So you're not coming back, are you?
Come on, it's just a joke, right?
Oh I know I will eventually find you
Hiding in the closet
With a grin big enough to
Shine light on the world's darkest corners
Could you smile on my heart right now?
As the realization sets in that
I no longer have the privilege
Of you saying, "It's open come on in"
Or wrapping your arms around me
While you laughed to the heavens
And made me know I was loved
It stings
It burns
It sucks
It hurts…but you're healed now
You're no longer bound to pain
Confusion, fears or doubts
And you are watching us as
You walk amongst the clouds
The sun peers through in those moments
I see you
I see your heart singing, but from so far away
Too distant for me to touch
I know that's the better place for you
But, you're not coming back, are you?

# Honesty Bit #3

Life is a rollercoaster filled with breathtaking mountain peaks and heartbreaking valleys. No matter what, sometimes we just have to learn to throw our hands up and enjoy the ride.

## Hands Up

Up above the clouds, so high
Euphoria turns into paranoia
Once we realize where we're headed
There's an uneasy feeling
At the pit of my stomach
And we anticipate this drop
No matter how hard we
Try to delay the inevitable
So there's nothing left to do
But throw our hands up
And try to make some fun
Through the fears
Create enough picture perfect snapshots
To sustain us through the tears
We'll always remember through the years
This uphill climb of this very moment
But what goes up
Must come down
This just isn't the way
I pictured our end to come about
And it seems there's
Nothing left to do but
Throw our hands up for the thrill
And close our eyes
Until we're able to
Meet again on the other side

# Did I Do That?

Does the calm collection of my emotions disturb you?
Does my well-read knowledge offend you?
Does it make you squirm in your seat?
Make you lose a little sleep
Overcome you till you weep
And capture your tongue
And make your teeth click
Tickle your vocal cords
Until you can't muster up a word to speak?
Tell me, does the very thought of it make you quiver
Shiver with fear because I am more
Than what you expected?
Better than what you professed me to be
Your quota ain't shit and has nothing on me
But you see, you fail to realize
You cannot calculate me
Just when you think I'll go right
That's when you'll find all you have left is the
Shattered pieces of what you thought you knew
And the lies you told yourself so much until
You thought they were true
Is my gaze abrasive to your soul?
Is my laugh a labyrinth you can't decode
Because you feel I couldn't possibly have
Anything to smile about?
Does my stance turn you on
Or make you wish you could turn her on like that?
Turn off your misconceptions, predetermined notions
And inferred conclusions
They have only left you with illusions of grandeur
That make you think you're more important than you really are
Does my presence offend you
Even when I'm not in the room?
I hope it does

## The One That Got Away

It's no secret that in relationships, we sometimes may feel like letting her or him go was the biggest mistake we ever could have made. For some people, they wallow in this feeling for years after the breakup. For others, it's simply just a short matter of time before they realize that walking away from a relationship was the best thing that could have happened to them. Whatever the case, we are unable to undo the past and the outcomes they created, no matter how hard we may try.

We have come to know "the-one-that-got-away" feeling as specifically concerning relationships. However, it goes much deeper than that. The one that got away can be related to a romantic love lost, but it also can mean a lost job opportunity, a dispute with a family member/friend and many other things. Is it devastating, depressing and a huge let down? Sure, it can be all of these things and even more. But at what point do we pick ourselves up off the floor?

The downside of throwing ourselves a pity party about whom or what we've lost is that all of the guests we invite slowly make their exit from our lives. Because we are so stuck on that person or thing, it makes the other person dealing with us have a headache and a half. We have to eventually get away from the thought of the one that got away if we ever want to move forward in life. So they got away? Maybe so, but you're still here. So what are you going to do to make the best of it?

## Blow Out The Candles

The flames sway and flicker in anticipation
Impatiently waiting for me to
Sequester their existence
Isn't it ironic that they
Seem to burn brighter
Right before the gust of wind
Turns them to ashes?
I wish to bring you back and
We could float in the atmosphere forever
That's selfish I know
I wish to finally let go of the
Things that make my hands bleed
Whenever I squeeze their jagged edges
I wish for my special occasion
Tomorrow to be light years
Ahead of what I celebrated yesterday
And more than I could ever hold today
Whatever that means
So close your eyes and
Make a wish
I miss that hot wax dripping
Just as we licked
The icing gripping so strongly
To our good times

## Am I The Only One?

Have you ever felt caged
While sitting in a wide open space?
Have you ever put on those facades
When underneath it all, everything was
Anything but ok?
Have you ever wanted to run away
With no questions, explanations
Or considerations for someone else's
Two cents that can't buy you out of your turmoil?
Have you ever looked at the sky
And thought the clouds have it easy
From up there while they look at us below
Scrambling trying to figure it all out?
Have you ever felt guilty to celebrate
Because everyone around you is drowning in sorrow?
Now you're fighting to stay afloat with them
Somebody pass me a life jacket
Before this tide comes surging in
Have you ever been given the
Key to freedom and just were afraid to use it
So the familiar sheets of uneasiness
Seem more logical to be tucked in to
Have you ever wanted to kick down the door
Separating you from clarity?
But then you realize there's nothing
There but you and open space….
And the echoes of your every thought

## Remove Your Cool

How many times has someone asked us, "How are you doing today?" and we respond with the generic, "I'm good, how about you?" Most people are polite enough to realize that everyone has their own problems and the last thing they want to do is take on someone else's. Wouldn't it be shocking if we asked people how they were doing and they actually told the truth? I know….a scary concept, right? A few months ago I found myself feeling a little blah for a few reasons, but I honestly didn't have the time to focus any energy on it. So I decided to do what many of us do at any given moment…fake it until you make it.

One of the greatest lessons I've learned this year is there is strength in your weakness. I'm the type of person that doesn't really like people to feel sorry for me (people that play up sympathy really irk me). Even if I'm sick, I usually just want to be by myself unless I'm just really out of commission. But sometimes, it's ok to admit that you don't feel good, you're pissed, disappointed or struggling with forgiveness. The best part about releasing the denial about our situations is that it helps free us from them. A victory can't be won without realizing the things that have the potential to defeat us.

Sometimes we just have to take off our cool to get to the real root of the problem. The first step is admittance and until we do that, we'll likely keep finding ourselves in the same rut. It's one thing to put on the front for other people, but it's a dangerous thing to start lying to yourself too. Are you holding on to your cool and hindering yourself in the process?

Take it off now (without going off on everyone around you – that's never a good idea) and don't worry about who it offends.

They will get over it. Don't worry about looking vulnerable either. You're still pushing through and haven't given up yet. Don't worry about tomorrow (or yesterday) and just live for today.

## Decisions

I decided….
Grace and fate collided
I tried and tried
And failed and lied
When it felt good to
Because that's what we're
Supposed to do, right?
I decided….
I would no longer fight it
Bullets flying, some I bite
While others strike like lightning
Just past the corners of my eye
Thank goodness for grace and fate
Colliding….
Cause my try was miles shy
Of what He can do
Glad He decided to give me another chance

## I Love You Only...

It's easy to love you
When the sun rises right
Above the small of your back
Right after we make love
It's easy to say I'll stay
When there are no arguments
And we agree to disagree
It's easy when the outside forces
Don't break down our barrier
We once held up so strongly
It's easy loving you
When I know you love me too
And don't have a glimpse of a wandering eye
I love you when you go along
With my wishes, my dreams, my fears, my needs
I love you when you aren't too head strong
And develop a mind on your own
But this love is tricky and things
Get sticky if you get too clingy
I love you just enough
To have one foot out the door
That gives me a head start on an easy escape
I love you when you're on my side
Right or wrong
Just on my terms
Because isn't that what love's all about?

## Heart Surgeon

Hurry, run quickly
It's an extreme emergency
I see your blood running to the floor
So I apply pressure firmly and then some more
But this gauze is soaked so crimson
I can't keep up
So I try to stitch it up and make
Your heart beat back to normal
Whatever that is
Just any state that's a precursor
To the break
And I would freeze time if I could
To make sure that moment never came
But time isn't so understanding
And love seems over complicated
And too demanding
Why can't it be simple?
Not flat lined like this
Wait, there's still some life left
But is it enough to carry us through?
Are you done and already gone? Am I too?
Your heart's in need of surgery
But there doesn't seem to be a remedy
Years from now it may just be a cool war wound
We'll have weathered the storm with brave hearts
But will we still be here to see the sun rise on
Your broken one?

## Not Oblivious

Put your hands down
Silence that tambourine now
We don't hear the joyful noise
Just gibberish and empty, selfish ploys
And that tattered and highlighted Bible
Has obviously been put to no use
So pass it down like hot potato
To someone who can better live its truths
We don't believe your testimony
Your whole persona reveals you're phony
Oh so that's what He told you to tell me?
I highly doubt it
And I don't need your strange hands
Oiled and pure from holy lands
Touching me
They're as dirty now as they were
When they left here
And I've never been fond
Of snakes praying for me
Sssssssssssooo…..you should move around
Pick up your face
Close your mouth
Unclench your fists
You are not in shock
You've felt this heat before
Just never quite this hot
You think no one sees
You laugh that no one knows
You think we're oblivious
But you're true color always show
We always knew you weren't loyal
Yep, just like the rest of those hoes….

# Honesty Bit #4

Happiness is temporary and changes with your mood. Joy is permanent and a conscious choice we make. Know the difference. Do you really just want to be happy?

# A Woman Named Joy

What is happiness to you and what does it really mean? Is it getting a promotion at work? Getting a new car? A new house? That beautiful woman or man you've had your eyes set on for months? Or maybe something as simple as a good meal at your favorite restaurant? There's nothing wrong with any of that, but there's one small problem: none of these things last forever. Anything new eventually gets old. That tight body will eventually wrinkle and sag over time. The foundation of that beautiful home can be destroyed if a strong enough storm hits it. So why be happy about anything at all?

Happiness is a wonderful thing, but something we shouldn't get too wrapped up in it. But why would anyone in their right mind turn down happiness? Because it never lasts. Happiness fits well into our microwave society because it's usually just quick gratification. The problem with happiness is that it's fickle. When happiness is at the pinnacle of its existence, so are we. But when the light of happiness is dim and hopelessly lit, there we are as well. Some of us go our whole lives chasing after happiness only to find in the end that we're chasing Band-Aids when what we needed all along was surgery.

Joy is beautiful, electrifying, caring, compassionate, understanding and best of all….lasting. If you pay close attention, you'll more than likely never hear someone say, "I had joy yesterday, but it's gone today". But too many times we say, "I was happy last week, but now I'm not". Joy doesn't mean that everything is necessarily going our way. Our tire may have just gone flat on the way to work. We may have just lost a loved one. We may have experienced a bad break up and living with the reality of it. But the woman named joy is still there, holding everything together like glue. Would you rather have the woman named Joy or the girl named Happiness? The choice is yours….

## Jealous Guys

The jealous guys
They make you smile and
Tingle between your knees
The jealous guys take the load
Off your shoulders and carry it
With ease
Those are the guys who know
How to get the party started
The ones that take you further
Than you ever dared to dream
The ones that know what to do
With your peaches and cream
Whipped, right into their hands
But you're too busy levitating
You're preoccupied, celebrating
This new thing that surely
No one else has ever experienced
You're elevated far beyond reality
Come back to the world before
It's too late
And you start making excuses like
I walked into the punch
And he's just got a heavy hand
It's just a little scar
And you're still his number 1 fan
The jealous guys
Have it so easy don't they
They call, you come
In more ways than one
They throw, you fetch
And we have the audacity to
Call them the dogs
That bark up the tree when your skirt
Is a Subway sandwich length above the knee
Foot long, dead wrong

Better heed the signs
Before you meet demise
At the hands of another ordinary jealous guy

## Principality

For principality you may have to ruffle some feathers
For principality you may have to be uncomfortable
Suffer some heart ache or be put back in your place
For principality you may have to bow down when your
Insides tell you to do everything but
Let principality guide you
In the long run it won't steer you wrong
For principality you just might have to
Do what you feel and ask for forgiveness later
Asking no permission, slip
And dip wherever the chips may fall
Because it's the principle of the matter
For principality, you may do the very thing you say you hate
Humble yourself and clean the crumbs around their plates
But there are exceptions and sometimes…
For principality, you just might have to whoop some ass…
And that's ok

# Doormat

I was once stunningly beautiful
Some would say immaculate
My splendid golds, royal blues
Regal purples and robust reds
Used to stop traffic for onlookers
To marvel in awe of my very creation
I was pretty secure back then
I knew myself back when
Life was as pure as the imported silk
That was woven to mold me
But somehow along the way I became
Gray, dingy, dirty and unclean
Now no one looks at me
And they just pass me by
No radiance or brilliance
Or sense of resilience
I've been reduced to a commoner
Just like the others
They knew I would be here
As they sneered and snickered
Awaiting my arrival
So many have found refuge in relieving
Dirt from their feet on me
Not giving a damn about what
It would do to my identity

## Open Secrets

The secret that screams
So loudly in the shadows is
The one we can't stomach
When the lights come on
Because we already know it's there
The writings are invisibly plastered on the walls
Somehow we fool ourselves into thinking
That the vultures swarming above us
Are nothing but mere feathers
Floating in the air
That just barely tickle our noses
Just enough for us to take notice
Yet and still, it's tolerable
There's just enough sweetness
To curb the gritty bitterness
But there's something to be said
For the unveiling of the space of
Claustrophobic truth we claim
We already knew…..
Yep….it sucks sometimes to know, doesn't it?

## Let's Play 'I Never'

One of my favorite games to play is a game called "I never". It's usually played with shots of some kind of alcohol, but nonalcoholic versions of the game are just as fun. The rules of the game are that everyone gets a turn to say something they've never done. If the other players have done that particular thing, they have to take a shot. Sounds simple enough right? However, as you may have already guessed, this game needs a time limit because it can literally go on for hours. It's interesting seeing how judgmental people become after a few rounds of playing the game.

Just like the game of 'I Never', we often times take shots (hypocritical jabs) at others for what they've done. I've pretty much always been the type of person to try not to pass judgment on people. Do I fall short at times? Heck yeah. I, just like all of us, have a stance on some issues/situations that can definitely come across as being judgmental. If I were to play 'I Never' today versus a couple of years ago, I'd be drinking to some things that I never (no pun intended) saw myself doing. Does that make me a bad person? No, it just makes me human and slaps me back into reality. We should caution against being so dead set on saying what we will or won't do.

Today, it may be easy to sit back while everyone else tips up their cup to lies, deceit, low self-esteem, cheating, fornication, murder and hate. If we're not the person that smokes marijuana, it's easy to call someone else to the carpet on it (while a flask is secretly tucked away in our back pocket). Consider yourself warned. The next time the cups go around, you just may be taking a sip too.

## Giving You The Finger

In my lifetime, I've had the chance to come in contact with some very wise people. One of those is the Pastor of my home church, Pastor Sylvester Duckens, Jr., PHD. I remember him giving a sermon one time and mentioning something about pointing fingers. I don't remember it all verbatim, but I do remember him saying that we should be careful of pointing fingers at other people. When we do, there are 3 pointing back at us. I didn't get it at first, but then it clicked. Whenever we literally point the finger at someone, 3 fingers are tucked back in our direction.

It's easy to place blame on other people for things that are going wrong in our lives. In fact, the blame seems to be rightfully placed in some instances. When someone has lied to us and we didn't do anything to prompt it, pointing the finger seems like the natural thing to do. But what do those three fingers pointing back at us really say? Have we dodged the bullet of lying but can't stop gossiping (which is usually based on some form of lies), using drugs or being hateful? Even if we have full right to give someone the finger, we shouldn't keep it out there too long. If we do, we run the risk of exposing those things within ourselves that people can give the finger to.

When we think about the physical action of pointing a finger, there is a part of our hand that's hidden. These are the three fingers pointing back at us. Just like those hidden fingers, we like to hide our flaws but call out the flaws of others. And to what advantage? To make ourselves feel better? The next time you give someone the finger, you may want to consider giving one to yourself too. What you find pointing back in your direction just may offend you.

## Tastes Like

She was their watermelon gum drop
Caramel butterscotch
Peachy cream cumquat
Cinnamon tinged Red Hot
Whatever flavor they craved
She quenched their desire
Whatever they wanted her to be
She allowed them to pluck all
The ripe fruit right off her tree
And she smiled as her juices
Glistened off their chins
She sighs deeply and breathes in...
Her sweet aroma of deception
Because she was their
Apple tart turnover pie
Their sweet plum sugary fairy
Their cherry picked
Ride or die chick
Prepared on a silver platter
Ever so tastefully
To their liking
But that's just it
She was so many flavors to so many men
That she forgot how the
True essence of her being really tasted

## Believer

I made you believe that these
Are my true colors
Changed up my identity like a chameleon
Creeping under your covers
Laid you down with
The seed to conceive
And give birth to thought
Of blurred lines of reality
And rational sensibility
Mirrors all around
And your own reflection
Is the last one you want to see
I've made you a believer
For longer than you can recount
How does it feel
To be a stranger in your own house?

## We Will Laugh

One day we will toss our
Heads back parallel to the sky
So high that our eyelashes kiss the clouds
Never mind them asking why
And we will laugh....
We'll laugh until our stomachs get so tight
And our eyes gleam so brightly with water
That washes away the past
We will feel the euphoric pounding in our chest
Like the deepest thump
Of a marching band bass drum
We will lose our voices over the joy
Drink hot totties to soothe the pain
And lose them some more
We will laugh beyond
Our heart's contentment
No room for resentment
We will laugh until we get too tired
To sit upright
Retire for the night
Wake up and do it all over again tomorrow
But today....ain't nobody laughing at anything

## Let My Shadow Be Enough

When words are not enough
To soothe the pain pouring from your soul
When a shoulder to lean on will not suffice
To give you strength to make your next step
When life throws you a curve ball
And you don't quite have the speed to catch it
If you question your very existence
And wonder where your worth is
If you stumble on slippery stones of the unknown
And need a retreat to catch your breath
If you're 5 miles to empty
And need some fuel along your path
When lies defy gravity
And truth seems galaxies away
When you are suspended in dissension
And have yet to find your freedom
When calamity fills your corridor
Let me walk by and at least
Give you a shadow
That will be more than what you need

## Up The Latter

I can't wait to get over the latter
They tell me how much of a joy it will be
And I can hear the jubilee
Eagerly anticipating me on the other side
But for now, I'm still climbing
I'm still digging
I'm still pulling
And I'm still struggling
Your latter will be greater
Is what they always say
But don't come to me with those
Helium infused affirmations that
You barely believe yourself
I'm not in the mood for it today
Up the latter will be better
Once I've already conquered
It will be sweeter once
I've already tasted victory
It will be much clearer
Once I can see it up close and personal
But would we ever really appreciate our latter
If we could cut it off at our discretionary pain points?
Keep climbing
Your latter is on the way

## Swerving In My Lane

With respect to keeping all things honest, I must admit that I have road rage at times. There are certain things drivers can do that really get me fired up. My biggest pet peeve is when another vehicle cuts in front of me and then decides to slow down. Come on now, if you must cut me off, at least step on the gas! To make matters worse, the driver usually isn't even going in the same direction I am. I find myself thinking, "Get out of my lane" (well, maybe not those exact words)! When it comes to competition with people in real life scenarios, why do some people insist on swerving in your lane?

Think about it. How many times have you been minding your own business, operating in your expertise or gift, and people are intimidated by it? I can be a competitive person when I want to be. But for the most part if the competition doesn't directly impact me, I'll let it slide. What really makes me laugh though is when people try to compete for something that's not a mutual goal for both parties involved. Let's say there are 2 people working on the same level at a job. One person wants to move on to a totally different department (and doesn't desire to be a people manager). The other person desperately wants to be a manager – at any cost. In a scenario like this, the person who desires to be the manager often gets jealous of the other person. This is despite the fact that the 2 people's aspirations are totally opposite.

I truly don't have the time or energy to compete over something that I don't even want. It's easy to get caught up in the competitive spirit. There's room for all of us at the top, contrary to popular belief. Some people just have a crab mentality though, and they can't wait to pull you back down as you climb up (even if they're truly content where they are). Wouldn't we all have so much more fulfillment out of life if we avoided swerving into other people's lanes?

## When The Screaming Stops

When the echoes of the last
"I hate you" resound the room
When I don't even care if you stay out
All night and come home in the afternoon
When I just agree to disagree
If it means you'll stop talking to me
When the fight has left the ring
And no one's willing to take an uppercut
When we hold our noses up high
Like we belong to the upper crust
Must we treat each other so coldly?
I guess so if you want to go
Then lock the door behind you
And don't look back because I won't
Come chasing after you
You find your own waterfalls
And I'll guide you downstream
When it's been day fifteen
And I don't miss you in my dreams
When we could care less
About the outcomes of the bluffs we call
And refuse to let our pride fall to the floor
Like those tears that we don't have anymore
When we let anger fester and multiply
During our slumber with no remorse
Can you hear the silence?
I kinda miss the chaotic verbal violence
But when all of these things
Begin to exit stage right
Houston, we have a problem
That won't get healed over night

## The Things We Never Said

Calling you out of your name
Is just a term of endearment
That means I really want you to stay
And stick around for at least one more day….or two
If you may please excuse me for
Saying you're not getting on my nerves
When in actuality I am pissed
And ticked to no end, again
You seem to be putting words in my mouth
Silence
Will you just let me speak?
Even if I don't have the slightest blues clue
Of what my next utterance will be
Why don't you understand me?
Maybe if we unpacked our intentions
And left room for what we always
Should have mentioned
Our better would be best
More no's would be a yes
And ambiguity would be put to eternal rest

## Slick Intuition

This intuition is causing friction
No intermissions and feels like
We're in need of an intervention
The tension commences to crawl under my skin
As ashes begin to fall
Near the sticks that rubbed on stones
That ignited the flame to shift the blame
That birthed the shame
You see this damn intuition cannot be tamed
And we are slaves shackled to
Its every move
Will it bleed us, drain us, teach us?
Or will it keep on searching until it seeks justice
Finding just us…..alone?

# Honesty Bit #5

Contrary to popular belief, there are just as many messy men as there are women. #ThatIsAll

## No M.A.M.

It's no secret that women are more than likely to be the gender that gossips about people more. Women are usually more catty and combative. This is why many groups of women eventually fall out. They are generally concerned with things (who is sleeping with who; who dresses better; who has better looking hair, etc) that men tend not to worry about. I'm no expert; this is just my opinion and experience with what I've seen in life. But ladies, there is hope yet. There are some pretty messy guys out there too. I've never understood the concept of focusing my energy on what someone else is saying or doing. Sure, I've said and done some things I shouldn't have when it comes to other people. But as long as people are happy, healthy and not harming themselves or others, I'm not too concerned.

The older I get, the more I realize there are some messy men out there too. We all have secrets, illnesses or tragedies that we may not want the whole world to know. I think it's nothing but fair for anyone to have that right. But too many times, I've heard men say (not necessarily directly to me) something like, "Yes, he's doing great despite the fact that he just got diagnosed with cancer". So what? Cancer is not a death sentence, and neither are any of the hardships or setbacks people may go through. The crazy thing about life is sometimes we can be put in the very situation (or worse) that we gossiped about someone else on.

It's one thing when a woman spreads someone else's business. It's almost to be expected. But there are just certain things a man shouldn't say when it comes to other people. Just like anyone else, we have a responsibility not to listen to certain things as well. If we just receive everything we hear, that makes us just as guilty as the person spilling the beans. So, the next time you hear a guy spilling someone else's business, just stop him and say, "No M.A.M." In case you're wondering what

"M.A.M." stands for the first M is for Messy and the last M is for Men. I'll let you guess what the A stands for.

## Phantom On the Run Neglecting (P.O.R.N.)

Creeping, tipping through the back door
Camouflaged in deceitful fatigues
The night time is the right time
Because the light of truth
Has never been your friend
But she let you in and that's
Where she went wrong
That's where you found wiggle room
To insert and slip and slide and
Stroke and poke and grope
And blast off to the mountain tops
To create this……child
And feeling of abandonment
You can look in their eyes
And easily see that yes
They need you
Yes, where were you
Besides the times you just wanted to
Come inside because it felt warmer there
The shelter from protection with no protection
Just left her responsible for
Being a care taker twice over
Once for the beautiful bundle of future resentment
In her arms and twice for….
For a grown ass man with a sippy cup in his hand
Drink up because this is the story of your life
Whether you object to accept your responsibility
The truth is you've disregarded their innocence
And forgotten the fact that they had
Nothing to do with what's love or lust or
Hate or mistrust has got to do with it
Don't speak now
You reveled in silence before
You had no problem with disappearing acts before
You had no issue ignoring their cries before

When you could have given even a little more
Don't speak now that you've reaped the harvest
Of your greatest performance ever
Headlining from city to city
You're just a phantom on the run neglecting
Everything in sight

## Snap Your Fingers

Snap Snap
It's time to wake up
Get up for the real turn up
We just slept through our breakthrough
Can you hear me though?
Snap your fingers if you really know
Snap snap
Since when did queens become
Synonymous with bitches?
But that's what he calls you
And that's what you answer to
So if you like it
I guess we're forced to love it too
You swallow lies as if they were the truth
Snap your fingers if you never knew
Snap snap
Injustice everywhere
And we turn deaf ears and blind eyes
Until we need someone to
Hear our own cries
Hash tags with no action
Will only spark useless fireworks
Forgetting our true worth
And call of duty
Snap snap
The hollow echoes of the spaces
We should have filled
Make it all the more grueling
But we're still snapping
And maybe we'll get it one day

## Pull These Strings

Every time I try to walk away
These cords keep pulling me back in
Even if I free fell away from you
Seems I would just snap back
And end up right back here with you
Every time you say you're leaving
I feel my heart shift
Ain't that some….
Never thought I'd be the one to
Be the vulnerable party
Who turned the lights out?
Love dims so bleakly down this hallway
As you walk closer
Sparks electrify
And the glow of my soul
Slowly comes back to life
I hate this codependency
But it seems it's the only way to be
Pulling each other's strings….

## Wonder Years

In the beginning
Things were cruising cool
We were running free and wild
Without a care
Wind blowing through our hair
Though mine is gone now
We stayed up late until
Our eyelids collapsed
Said we wouldn't do it again
But longed for the relapse
We said what we felt
And left no apologizes
Tip toed to the edge
No matter how dangerously it felt
Like ice cream truck
Goodies we'd race outside to eat
Sun melting down our backs
As we walked down
What seemed to be a never ending street
Innocence, now gone
Now we are aware of time, space, and restriction
We are not free in our skin
And strapped to other people's opinions
Too conscious of image
Losing ourselves in the abyss
Who knew growing up
Would ever feel like this?
No time for pleasure
And priorities are skewed
Climbing up the ladder
But we never reach the roof
Can somebody send
That ice cream truck my way?
I could use a break today
These wonder years were wonderful

Until we fully grew out of them
Abandoning naivety
If I knew they would have passed this fast
I would have never let go of them

## Your Hood Won't Save You

You are the most influential
Rocking chair activist
Man has ever known
Fist pump that
Yet your feet never
Touch the ground
Rocking and complaining
Wallowing in complacency
Confused with cooling waters
That soothe your mind and help you
Sleep at night because you've
Really made a difference
And just to prove your stance for injustice
You've posted a new profile pic
On every social media outlet
With a hooded head shot
With the hash tag #RealMenStandUp
You smile, with satisfaction, as you log out
They laugh when they log in
Because your hood will not save you
Your silent militancy is unwavering
Little boys in Tennessee cannot benefit
From your shallow jubilee
They cannot feel the impact of your
Hooded swaggerific sweatshirt
While you were pulling your head through it
Another shot was fired in the night
Where were you?
Another body falls helplessly to the ground
Did you answer the call?
Another family is left to grieve
Why aren't we following you?
You can keep your hood
Just know this is true

It won't save them
Any more than it saves you

## Just Between Me And You

Can you keep a secret? When was the last time someone trusted you with something personal that they didn't want to get out? Did you keep it to yourself or did you tell someone else? We've all been on the receiving and giving end of secrets. No matter who you are, you have some kind of secret or personal issue that you don't want the whole world to know. So the question arises of who can we really trust? Almost no one. Right now you may be shaking your head and thinking I'm a negative person, but I'm really not. That is just the truth. Think about it. How many times have you been the victim of or heard about someone supposedly keeping a secret that leaked to their one best friend? Then that friend tells their best friend, and so on and so forth.

It's never a good thing to spread someone else's business. But sometimes we have to sit back and ask ourselves how much ammunition we've given to others. Are we being too free with information that we maybe should have kept to ourselves? Unfortunately I've had to learn this the hard way. There have been certain friends that I've mentioned things to and then I later heard about it. And everyone knows what happens when a story gets passed down. There's a little twist each time it's handed off. By the time it gets back to you, the whole scenario has changed.

Am I saying that we should keep everything to ourselves and not vent to anyone? Not at all. Most of us have at least one or two friends/family members who are trustworthy enough to stop the information passing when it gets to them. We would be much better off if we just tell that person and leave it at that. At the end of the day, it's not worth the frustration and tarnished friendship. Those things that we say are "just between me and you" should sometimes really be between us and God.

## Honesty Box

Within these 4 walls lies
Bitter judgment
Beautiful healing
Unwavering acceptance
Exhilarating epiphanies
Stubborn ideals
Staggering defeats
Shattering truths
Appealing lies
And eyes to see beyond
The screens
Between the lines
Their silent cries are seldom heard
Reaching out to millions
With just one click
But who's really paying attention?
No one
It's not on their agenda
But with the turn of this key
It unlocks
The greatest unsolved mysteries
The most joyous reunions
We'll see each other again some day
Won't we?
The words and thoughts and actions
And feelings and emotions
Spewing out of this box are real
So open if you dare
Explore if you must
Don't mind the dust
It's been a while since we've
Had some company
So make yourself at home

## Not Amused

I paid the inexpensive cost to
Enter this amusement park
Little did I know that by the time I left
There would be no change in my pockets
And anything but amusement left in my heart
All of the rides, food and games
Provided hours and hours of entertainment
Was that the limit of my existence?
A mere show to be performed on the stage?
Whatever the case
I must not ever come here again
One visit is enough
One experience is too much
And nothing here is as enticing
As the freedom that its gates escape to
Unveiled, this is self-destruction at its best
Because it was not the park owner
All the rides, food and games
That gave my mind away
It was when I decided to stay instead
Of wave and drive by

## Dead End Street

I'm staring at this wall
Foot mashed on the brake
I open the door to get some fresh air
Only to step out in the rain
I claw at these concrete barricades
Until my hands become blood soaked
There's life all around me
But I can't feel it
Because the silence of my reality
Is screeching so loudly
That it's smothering
I knew this day would come
But didn't expect it
To feel quite like this
I just can't help but think
There's another chapter waiting
Here beyond these bricks
That I can't tear down
Might as well turn around
But I feel I've come too far
To turn back now
So perhaps there's a blessing in
My pressing and feeling like
I haven't moved an inch
If I reached the other side
Tell me what is beyond these bricks?

## That Self $^!t

You're so stuck in your stench
Beyond scratch and sniff
Of that self...ish....ness
Your sense of smell is shot to....
It has become your existence and
The very meaning of your being
Only thinking of yourself
Never anyone else
It's gonna get you
It's gonna catch you
Karma will boomerang and
Lay you flat on your back eventually
And all of those that you mistreated
Will stand over you snickering
As they should
As you would
As you struggle....defeated
Wallowing in the dirty, muddy, stinky, slippery
Self....ish...ness
You're so full of that self $^!t
That you probably think this poem is about you
And you're right....it is

# Honesty Bit #6

Don't let the mistakes of yesterday hinder your promises for today.

## I Might Be

Yes, I may have inhaled a time or two
Or drank way past my limit
When I knew I wasn't supposed to
May have mismanaged some funds
Bounced a few checks and even
Taken a few of your prized possessions
That didn't belong to me
But I wanted them and they were mine
At least for the time being
Easy come, easy go I guess
And I might have become involved with
The kind of crowd that
People cringe to see coming
But really, we don't mean any harm
We just command respect by any means necessary
And trust that we'll get it
I may have a few orange jumpsuits in my closet
That and some other things that may come spilling out
If I open this door and decide to let you inside
I may have questioned my worth at times
Even when I knew I was better than that
I could have had more sexual partners than
You have fingers and toes and cars and clothes
I may have done all of these things
Or none of the above
But some of us love to play God
And sit at the throne and judge
Just because I may have done it
Doesn't mean I need intervention
I didn't know I needed permission……
To be human
If you haven't done it yet
You will….just keep living

## Good Thing I Don't....

You know, it's really a good thing
I don't do drugs
Cause right about now, dealing with you
I'd be stoned out of my head like Macy Gray
In a misty, purple haze for days
And they could just leave me be
And for once give me some space to contemplate
And you know, it's a really good thing
I don't own a gun
Cause right about now, if I did
I'd fire off random warning shots
To get them to all settle down
To get them to all shut up
And get out of my face with their demands
And it's a really good thing
I don't drink, well not more than socially
Cause at this very moment
I can taste myself buying out the bar
Give me all the bottles off the wall
If you won't, then I will
Slurred speech, but it's real
The things we do to cope
When we feel we can't deal
When we know eventually
Everything will be just fine
But eventually often takes too much time
And sometimes it seems more logical
To just be out of your mind

## By Invitation Only

Birthday parties, weddings, VIP areas of a club and even some funerals are a few examples of events we need invitations to attend. There's something special about an invitation that makes you feel important. Have you ever thought that the negative and positive energy in our lives works the same way? We pray to God for Him to bless all of our new-found resolutions for the year. Increase my territory. Increase my finances. Decrease my weight. Give me a raise. Give me a new house. The list goes on and on. We are greedy by nature and the more we get, it seems like the more we want. But there just may be a way to get the things we really want out of life.

Imagine getting invited to a private party. You get freshened up, pull out your most trendy clothes, and get ready for the time of your life. Only to find out that when you arrive at the party, the person throwing it slams the door in your face. You look puzzled and don't understand how you received the invite, but the host treated you with such disrespect. This is exactly what we do to God when we speak negativity into the requests we beg and plead for. How can we really expect to land that dream job when we tell everyone, "Maybe I'm just not qualified enough". It's always wise to be truthful to your own self. But there's a fine line between being true to you and speaking defeat over yourself. Speaking negativity into the very things we say we want just delays the process, and shuts the doors of possibility.

No one likes having the door slammed in their face. So why do we feel so comfortable praying about the things we want and then speaking negatively over them? We are essentially slamming the door of opportunity for us in God's face. Great things can still come to us, even if we do speak negatively, but it's a great idea to make the process as easy as possible. Don't invite the blessings you say you desire with all of your heart…..only to speak doubt into them by your actions and words. The party is waiting for you and you've already received the invitation. Expect the best and get ready to have the good time you deserve. Don't revoke your invitation to the best life you could ever live.

## Drip Drop Floods

A few months ago, before my wife and I moved in together, the toilet in my apartment was dripping water from the valve. I only noticed it when I was at home by myself and everything was off – no TV or radio. I kept hearing a soft splashing noise of water hitting ground. I realized it was coming from my toilet and there was a small puddle of water on the floor. After attempting to fix it myself (with no luck), I decided to let my apartment complex know about it.

Of course, it happened on a Saturday when maintenance was technically off duty. But I told them it should be manageable enough to wait until Monday. After getting frustrated with transferring soaked towels to my washer, I put a small pot right under the valve and just lined some other towels around it. Seems simple enough, right? Well, the next morning I walked into the bathroom to brush my teeth and stepped into a puddle of water. I looked down and the entire floor was wet.

Something that started out as a small drip had turned into a mini flood. Isn't it funny how life can be just like that dripping flood? We can see the problem staring us right in the face and think that we can always patch it up with excuses, denial or poor preparation. Sure, this works for the short term. But it will never hold up forever. Stop the leak now, before it turns into a flood you can't control.

## Forever Ain't Far

Favor ain't fair
And neither are we
Shooting verbal daggers
Break ups to make ups
Just reconcile and in the end
Say we're sorry
Sleeping under the bridge
Below zero, we're so cold
Wind chill factor makes
Our soul's light low
Blow their candles out
Before it's time
But what we think is too short
Was calculated so divinely
Doesn't it hurt to think
Forever is full of too many possibilities?
Only one to choose
Only one we want
Can't fake the funk
Either you do or don't
Forever is what you make it
Right now
And sometimes it ain't
What we thought it would be

## N2MeUC (Intimacy)

One too many is still not enough
Poked so many notches in this belt
Until my pants are slipping off
To the floor where they like to stay
And I have nothing left to wear
Naked silhouettes, switching places
Changing faces
Exchange my kiss for your kiss
My grip for your scratches
My push for your pull
My insecurities for your insanity
Now we're all stirred up in this boiling pot
Of sweaty bodily fluids
Wondering where we went wrong
What's my name again?
Who did you tell me you were?
Tussling the sheets off the bed
And as the last echo of pleasure
Fills the air
So does the cold stillness
Of the lack of intimacy….
Damn, there was nothing really there

## One Up

Remember the old school Mario Brothers games where you grab the mushroom and get one up in size? That's the way many of us treat our lives and interactions with other people. That's why reality TV has become so overwhelmingly popular now. We look at these people who are 9 times out of 10 acting out a script and think, "My situation isn't anywhere near as bad as theirs". So we puff up our chests and feel as though we have a one up on everyone else. What a mistake we've made...

The funny thing people don't realize when they are "spilling the dirt" is the person listening often has dirt on them too. I guess no one really has an up on anybody then, do they? But many of us live in a fantasy world where we think we know everyone else's business and no one knows anything about our own. Again, what a mistake we've made. You may have a one up on somebody because you know something about them that they wouldn't want you to know. But chances are that very same person knows three things about you that you wouldn't want people to know.

So how about we just leave the one ups for the video games? Many times it may make us feel better about ourselves to have the so called upper hand on a person or a situation. But is that one up really just a Band-Aid to mask our flaws? That's a question that has to be answered individually. Are we so quick to tell about someone losing their job, to hide the fact that we got so drunk last week that we woke up in a strange room with our pants down? Or are we making fun of someone's failed marriage when our kids are so out of control that the mother, father, grandparents and pastor can't even get them in line? Let's not worry about the one ups and focus on us instead of somebody else.

## Insomniac

Does it dance atop your eyelids
In the night, under the twilight stars?
Does it alarm you ever so slightly?
With the chaotic clamor
And remind you that your existence is
Kept prisoner, behind bars
Does it cast a dark shadow on your most
Vibrant pictorial?
Does it hurt and feel so devastating
That you'd rather not
Be coherent enough to know?
Does it make you toss and turn
And burn and yearn for that
Touch that you'll never get back?
Does it leave you with a tingling sensation
Of regret, remorse, reform?
Of course….it does
Who are we really fooling?
I know it but I just want to hear
You utter the words and speak it
Tell me how it feels
To walk a day in your shoes
Tell me all about the agony of how it
Must feel to be you

## Wipped

Don't mind me and all this debri
Watch your step
And sift through to see
If you can create a make shift seat
Don't you dare point that
Judgmental finger at me
I drink, I smoke, I sex, I love
I sex some more…and drink some more
Watch me do it with no hands
But I can come as I am
Says my Savior up above
These piercing needles etching
Picturesque clasping hands
These pants that grip the cuff of my ass
Running down the aisles
Giving my best praise dance
These fists that assault and caress
And apologize to make room
For the next time I do it again
But it's ok because I'll still get in…right?
These abused chemicals
That alter my thought process
On this altar
These machetes that escape my lips
Which I claim I have no control of
These grand all expenses unpaid
Guilt trips I take those I love on
But go on and shake your head
In disgust if you must
I'm a work in progress

And in Him I trust
Slowly but surely
We'll get there if we just try

## Better You Than Me

I have a friend that lives by the saying, "Better you than me". When I first heard it, I thought it was a little cruel. But over time, it has made so much more sense to me now. It basically means that you're not being heartless, but someone else should lose sleep over something instead of you. Life has a way of bringing experiences to our lives that may make us debate about telling someone how we truly feel. But then there are those that don't debate anything (or so it seems) and just shoot from the hip.

We may look at people that are too direct and call them bossy, direct, over bearing or even other words that are too explicit to mention here. But one thing we surely won't say about those kinds of people is that they let people walk over them. They don't lose sleep over much because they get everything off their chest at the time that they feel it. Another thing I noticed about people who say what they feel (even if it lacks couth) is that they are less likely to hold grudges. A person who is not hesitant to tell someone off usually says what they have to say and then they are done with it. Maybe there's some good in shifting uncomfortable feelings to other people after all...

So what's the point of the "better you than me" mindset? You may be thinking that it's simply a green light to go ballistic on someone whenever we feel like it. But that's the furthest thing from the truth. The reality is when we are able to release those negative thoughts from our minds, our lives run much smoother. Think about it. Imagine coming in to work and your boss criticizes you for the things they don't even know how to do if they tried. You hold everything in and never bring this to their attention. It could be because of fear, being polite or avoiding confrontation. Meanwhile, you start to develop health problems and can't figure out why you need a glass of wine to sleep every night. The answer is simple….and cheap. Just say what you feel. Believe me; I'm still working on this one myself. But if we take on the "better you than me" attitude, we'll all feel a whole lot better about life. Worst case scenario is people won't like what is said or done. But they will definitely get over it. And if they don't, it never was your cross to bear anyway.

## Beautiful Trouble

I usually don't do this
But for you I will
For the thrill, I will
Like riding with the top down
With birds swarming above your head
Hoping you don't poop on me
But it's worth the rush and dodging the possibility
I'm walking through a maze of landmines
Not saying I'll catch a grenade for you though
Tick...tick...boom...bam....pow!
Like those old Batman flicks
Don't you explode on me
Riding the pinnacle of these waves
As they propel me further
And further away from the shore
But I'm not scared
There's a lighthouse somewhere out here
I can smell this beautiful trouble cooking
So intoxicating of an aroma you are
Dizzy with disillusion
Mesmerized by such a marvelous wonder
Time will tell who's right or who's wrong
Either way, your trouble looks so damn good to me

## Pillow Talk

Lay your head on my pillow
Whether it's raining in southern California
Or sunny in Massachusetts
Let's lose our cool cloaks
And loose our inhibitions
And burn the rubber on intellectual
Conversation until we begin to lose tread
Nevermind, I'm just playing
That was just something I said
To get you in this bed
And she says lay your head on my pillow
Let me dig my nails so far into your back
Till your skin starts to split
In some twisted, uplifting, instant vintage
But futuristic sort of way
And by the way
When we finish can you take me shopping?
I know I'm not your baby
But Bebe is having a sale I can't miss
He thinks ain't this some...
As the credit card swipes
Real love declined
Yet they don't seem to mind
The games we play just
To have someone's head lay on a pillow
Are we pillow talking
Like the old days when we
Envied Cliff and Claire Huxtable?
They seemed to have it all together
Or are we just talking sh!t
Pulling out fast
And sliding quick......ly
Lying to get what we want?

## Check Your DM (Direct Message)

I've been waiting 56 days and counting
I ended my last message with LOL
But this is no laughing matter
I really need you to respond
I know you've seen it because
The time stamp told me so
Better find someone else to
Play your fool because it won't be me
One day you'll need me
One day you'll wait for me to respond
And I'll purposely ignore your message
And answer everyone else's with glee
Oh say can you see how technology
Has made me such an effective communicator
At least in my mind
No really, how many people have you
Sent that picture to of your behind?
Check your DM in the PM
If you're stretched too thin in the AM
The requiem of a dream
Where we all pick up the phone
Instead of messaging the
Things we're just too scared to say
Seems to dissipate in the dust
Of direct message irony
Like spoons for salads
Common sense that doesn't mix
Put a fork in our communication for now
As I wait patiently for your response

## Smooth Skin

How do you glide effortlessly above the ground
With such an infectious glow?
Bruised, battered, bent and broken
Yet, no one ever knows
So tell me what's your secret?
Because we've all been privy to your pain
Your flawless naked body
Shows it was never endured in vain
They all want to reach out and touch
They lust and admire and marvel and inquire
See they are riddled with scars and can't comprehend
How beauty could transpire from
Times when faith is such a distant friend
Not knowing all along this glow
Radiates from within
Maybe a subtle caress
Will make us all feel comfortable too
As we undress and unlock these handcuffs
Baring it all, no longer oppressed
Whipped, punched, slapped and slammed to the floor
Yet you stand beautifully defiant
Skin so smooth
Skin so soft
Skin so supple
Skin so damn tough
No black and blue hues
Skin so beautiful
And it looks nothing like
What you've been through

## Quicksand

Sticking my toe in
Just abreast the surface
Careful not to fully step in
Because I know you'll swallow me whole
Sinking slowly, slipping deeper
Finders keepers, losers weepers
Ain't nobody crying
Maybe I like being captured
You were so confident
Playing the predator
You didn't consider maybe I
Was your willing prey
You'll get it on your way home
I like it better that way
True, you are the quicksand
I slipped and sloshed and slithered
My way into
But was it really by your traps
Or my recognition of like forces
That always repel
And found it easy for me to rebel
You yell but can anybody hear?
I am you and you are me
So who's really losing grip
In this quicksand fantasy?

## Why We Lie

We lie because the truth
Knocks us flat on our ass
Because it's harder to see through
Smudged and finger printed glass
We lie because the truth
Is as bitter as boiled bark from a tree
While lies are a delectable Tahitian treat
Like Jello there's always room for one
And they go down nice and easy
We lie because
We don't want to see that
Waning look of disappointment spread across your face
Because we know if we told the truth
We'd have to be put in our rightful place
Oh what a disgrace
So we dodge that curved bullet
Like Angelina Jolie
The truth is something we all
Enjoyed as a youth
When we were naïve and starry eyed enough
To believe that for everything, there was proof
Truth that doesn't sting, scratch or bleed
A beautiful pasture without the presence of weeds
But then we grew up
And we lied to impress
We lied to undress
We lied under stress
We'd probably still lie even if
We weren't under duress
But at best a lie is our Savior
That is dependable at each interval
Of doubt, confusion and fear
And at worst
It's the ship that throws us overboard
Into a lake named Deceit that

Feeds into an ocean called Delusion
With no life jacket
But relax....it's just a lie, right?

## Keep Your Fame

I never really wanted to be famous
That kinda stuff fades like modern day
Children putting down Legos and picking up iPads
At some point, it all becomes a thing of the past
Wasted and washed away from shore
Faded and blurred from clear view
I don't need clairvoyance to see into the future that
The pain of the pop life pushes
Purpose and true intentions out of the window
But so many people want to go
They'll sell their souls to get
A slice of the pie
And then scream to the heavens
Once they realized someone must have
Messed up their order
Oops... maybe it was a self-inflicted cataclysm
It wasn't supposed to be like this
Only euphoria and liberating bliss
I don't want to be famous
Really I don't
You may not think it's true
But I'd rather be that wind that
Hits your left ear ever so slightly
And makes you smile
I want to be that spark lit
From the firecracker that
Lights up your eyes with delight
I want to be that feeling of the best joke
You've ever heard
The kind when you

Laugh for days afterwards
And your stomach hurts from the fun you had
I want to be that cup of coffee
You wouldn't dare do without
In the morning
I want to be that rolling avalanche
That ignites you to run towards your dreams for safety
You can keep your fame
And name in neon lights
I'd much rather be remembered

# Honesty Bit #7

*She's one tough cookie that you can't resist and she's got a big secret that's about to be revealed.*
*#ComingSoon*

## Fortune Cookie

The novel about a woman that men love and women love to hate. She's got a shameful secret that has never been revealed to anyone….until now.

I can feel the jealousy burning through me with their stares. But I don't mind it. It actually makes me tingle down below to know that I've beat the odds yet again. I thrive on the impossible and this is just another example of the tables turning in my favor. It hasn't always been easy, but it's damn sure been worth every minute of it. I smile and sway, gliding ever so gracefully along my path. My hips are spread just right. My breasts naturally rise to the occasion and this one suits me oh so well. My ass is firmly accentuated just enough to let them know I've still got it. Yes, this dress fits me like a glove and I look stunning. No Spanks either.

Ok…..breathe. I've got to get focused again and back to the task at hand. Can I really bring myself to do this? Funny how you can see the wrongs in everyone else's life but be blind for so long when it comes to righting your own wrongs. Am I really deserving of such an honor? What would these people think if they were introduced to the real me? Something feels strange now and the walls are beginning to close in on me. Suddenly I'm seeing things that shouldn't be here and my stomach feels queasy.

My confidence is deflating with each step. My ankles feel as though I'm walking in water with 20 pound weights. My poker face is always on point, but I think they can tell something is not right. Shit! This is the most inopportune time for this. Everything is getting so blurry. My knees are getting weak and I can feel my head pounding as I hit the floor. Please God, somebody save me…..

www.ingramcontent.com/pod-product-compliance
Lightning Source LLC
Chambersburg PA
CBHW020659300426
44112CB00007B/450